Of the Work of Monks

Of the Work of Monks

St. Augustine

Of the Work of Monks

© Lighthouse Publishing 2018

Written by: St. Augustine (Nov.13 354 – Aug.28 430)

Translated by: Rev. H. Browne, M.A.

Updated into Modern U.S English by A.M. Overett (b. 1960)

All rights reserved. Without limiting the rights under copyright reserved above, no part of this publication may be reproduced, stored in a retrieval system, or transmitted, in any form or by any means (electronic, mechanical, photocopying, recording or otherwise), without the prior written permission of the copyright owner of this book.

Published by
Lighthouse Christian Publishing
SAN 257-4330
5531 Dufferin Drive
Savage, Minnesota, 55378
United States of America

www.lighthousechristianpublishing.com

Introductory Notice.

From the Retractations, ii. 21. To write the Book on the Work of Monks, the need which compelled me was this. When at Carthage there had begun to be monasteries, some maintained themselves by their own hands, obeying the Apostle; but others wished so to live on the oblations of the faithful, that doing no work whence they might either have or supply the necessaries of life, they thought and boasted that they did rather fulfill the precept of the Gospel, where the Lord saith, Behold the fowls of heaven, and the lilies of the field, (Matt. vi. 26). Whence also among laics of inferior purpose, but yet fervent in zeal, there had begun to arise tumultuous contests, whereby the Church was troubled, some defending the one, others the other part. Add to this, that some of them who were for not working, wore their hair long. Whence contentions between those who reprehended and those who justified the practice, were, according to their party affections, increased. On these accounts the venerable old Aurelius, Bishop of the Church of the same city, desired me to write somewhat of this matter; and I did so. This Book begins, "Jussioni tuæ, sancte frater Aureli." This work is placed in the Retractations next after that "On the Good of Marriage" which belongs to the year 401.

St. Augustine

1. Thy bidding, holy brother Aurelius, it was meet that I should comply withal, with so much the more devotion, by how much the more it became clear unto me Who, out of thee, did speak that bidding. For our Lord Jesus Christ, dwelling in thine inner part, and inspiring into thee a solicitude of fatherly and brotherly charity, whether our sons and brothers the monks, who neglect to obey blessed Paul the Apostle, when he saith, "If any will not work, neither let him eat," are to have that license permitted unto them; He, assuming unto His work thy will and tongue, hath commanded me out of thee, that I should hereof write somewhat unto thee. May He therefore Himself be present with me also, that I may obey in such sort that from His gift, in the very usefulness of fruitful labor, I may understand that I am indeed obeying Him.

2. First then, it is to be seen, what is said by persons of that profession, who will not work: then, if we shall find that they think not aright, what is meet to be said for their correction? "It is not," say they, "of this corporal work in which either husbandmen or handicraftsmen labor, that the Apostle gave precept, when he said, 'If any will not work, neither let him eat.'" For he could not be contrary to the Gospel, where the Lord Himself saith, "Therefore I say unto you, be not solicitous for your life, what ye shall eat, neither for your body, what ye shall put on. Is not the life more than meat, and the body than raiment? Consider the fowls of heaven, that they sow not, nor reap, nor gather into barns; and your heavenly Father feeds them. Are not ye rather of more worth than they? But who of you by taking thought can add to his stature one cubit? And concerning raiment, why are ye solicitous? Consider the lilies of the field, how they

grow; they labor not, neither spin; but I say unto you, that not even Solomon in all his glory was arrayed like one of these. But if the grass of the field, which today is, and tomorrow is cast into the oven, God so clothes; how much more you, (O ye) of little faith! Be not therefore solicitous, saying, What shall we eat, or what shall we drink, or wherewithal shall we be clad? for all these things do the Gentiles seek. And your heavenly Father knows that ye need all these. But seek ye first the kingdom of God, and His righteousness, and all these shall be added unto you. Be not therefore solicitous for the morrow: for the morrow will be solicitous for itself. Sufficient unto the day is the evil thereof." Lo, say they, where the Lord bids us be without care concerning our food and clothing: how then could the Apostle think contrary to the Lord, that he should instruct us that we ought to be in such sort solicitous, what we shall eat, or what we shall drink, or wherewithal we shall be clothed, that he should even burden us with the arts, cares, labors of handicraftsmen? Wherefore in that he saith, "If any will not work, neither let him eat;" works spiritual, say they, are what we must understand: of which he saith in another place, "To each one according as the Lord hath given: I have planted, Apollos hath watered; but God gave the increase." And a little after, "Each one shall receive his reward according to his own labor. We are God's fellow-workers; God's husbandry, God's building are ye: according to the grace which is given unto me, as a wise master builder I have laid the foundation." As therefore the Apostle worketh in planting, watering, building, and foundation-laying, in that way whoso will not work, let him not eat. For what profited in eating spiritually to be fed with the word of God, if he do not thence work others' edification? As that slothful servant, what did it profit to receive a talent and to hide it, and not work for the Lord's gain? Was it that it should be taken from him at last, and himself cast into outer darkness? So, say they, do we also. We read with the brethren, who come to us fatigued from the turmoil of the world, that with us, in the word of God, and in prayers, psalms, hymns, and spiritual songs, they may find rest. We speak to them, console, exhort, building up in them whatever unto their life, according to their degree, we perceive to be lacking. Such works if we wrought not, with peril should we receive of the Lord our spiritual sustenance itself. For this is it the Apostle said, "If anyone will not work, neither let him eat." Thus do these men deem themselves to comply with the apostolic and evangelic sentence, when both the Gospel they believe to have given precept concerning the not caring for the corporal and temporal indigence of this life, and the Apostle concerning spiritual work and food to have said, "If any will not work, neither let him eat."

3. Nor do they attend to this, that if another should say, that the Lord indeed, speaking in parables and in similitudes concerning spiritual food and clothing, did warn that not on these accounts should His servants be solicitous; (as He saith, "When they shall drag you to judgment-seats, take no thought what ye shall speak. For it will be given you in that hour what ye shall speak: but it is not ye that speak, but the Spirit of your Father that speaks in you." For the discourse of spiritual wisdom is that for which He would not that they should take thought, promising that it should be given unto them, nothing solicitous thereof;) but the Apostle now, in manner Apostolical, more openly discoursing and more

properly, than figuratively speaking, as is the case with much, indeed well-nigh all, in his Apostolic Epistles, said it properly of corporal work and food, "If any will not work, neither let him eat:" by those would their sentence be rendered doubtful, unless, considering the other words of the Lord, they should find somewhat whereby they might prove it to have been of not caring for corporal food and raiment that He spoke when He said, "Be not solicitous what ye shall eat, or what ye shall drink, or wherewithal ye shall be clothed." As, if they should observe what He saith, "For all these things do the Gentiles seek;" for there He shows that it was of very corporal and temporal things that He spoke. So then, were this the only thing that the Apostle has said on this subject, "If any will not work, neither let him eat;" these words might be drawn over to another meaning: but since in many other places of his Epistles, what is his mind on this point, he most openly teaches, they superfluously essay to raise a mist before themselves and others, that what that charity advises they may not only refuse to do, but even to understand it themselves, or let it be understood by others; not fearing that which is written, "He would not understand that he might do good."

4. First then we ought to demonstrate that the blessed Apostle Paul willed the servants of God to work corporal works which should have as their end a great spiritual reward, for this purpose that they should need food and clothing of no man, but with their own hands should procure these for themselves: then, to show that those evangelical precepts from which some cherish not only their sloth but even arrogance, are not contrary to the Apostolical precept and example. Let us see then whence

the Apostle came to this, that he should say, "If any will not work, neither let him eat," and what he thereupon joined on, that from the very context of this lesson may appear his declared sentence. "We command you, brethren, in the name of our Lord Jesus Christ, that ye withdraw yourselves from every brother that walked unquietly, and not according to the tradition which they have received of us. For yourselves know how ye ought to imitate us; for we were not unquiet among you, neither ate we bread of any man for naught, but in labor and travail night and day working that we might not burden any of you: not for that we have not power, but that we might give ourselves as a pattern to you in which ye should imitate us. For also when we were with you, we gave you this charge, that if any will not work, let him not eat. For we have heard that certain among you walk unquietly, working not at all, but being busy-bodies. Now them that are such we charge and beseech in our Lord Jesus Christ, that with silence they work, and eat their own bread." What can be said to these things, since, that none might thereafter have license to interpret this according to his wish, not according to charity, he by his own example hath taught what by precept he hath enjoined? To him, namely, as to an Apostle, a preacher of the Gospel, a soldier of Christ, a planter of the vineyard, a shepherd of the flock had the Lord appointed that he should live by the Gospel; and yet himself exacted not the pay which was his due, that he might make himself a pattern to them which desired what was not their due; as he saith to the Corinthians, "Who goes a warfare at any time at his own charges? Who planted a vineyard, and of its fruit eat not? Who fed a flock, and of the milk of the flock partakes not?" Therefore, what was due to him, he would not receive, that by his example they might be checked, who, although not so ordained in the Church, did deem the like to be due to themselves. For what is it that he saith, "Neither ate we bread of any man for naught, but in labor and travail night and day working that we might not burden any of you; not for that we have not power, but that we might give ourselves as a pattern to you wherein ye should follow us?" Let them, therefore, hear to whom he hath given this precept, that is, they which have not this power which he had, to wit, that while only spiritually working they should eat bread by corporal labor not earned: and as he says, "We charge and beseech in Christ that with silence they work and eat their own bread," let them not dispute against the most manifest words of the Apostle, because this also pertained to that "silence" with which they ought to work and eat their own bread.

5. I would, however, proceed to a more searching and diligent consideration and handling of these words, had I not other places of his Epistles much more manifest, by comparing which, both these are made more clearly manifest, and if these were not in existence, those others would suffice. To the Corinthians, namely, writing of this same thing, he saith thus, "Am I not free? am I not an Apostle? Have I not seen Christ Jesus our Lord? Are not ye my work in the Lord? If to others I am not an Apostle, to you assuredly I am. For the seal of mine Apostleship are ye in the Lord. My defense to them which interrogate me is this. Have we not power to eat and to drink? Have we not power to lead about a woman who is a sister, as also the other Apostles, and the brethren of the Lord, and Cephas?" See how first he shows what is lawful to him,

and therefore lawful for that he is an Apostle. For with that he began, "Am I not free? am I not an Apostle?" and proves himself to be an Apostle, saying, "Have I not seen Christ Jesus our Lord? Are not ye my work in the Lord?" Which being proved, he shows that to be lawful to him which was so to the other Apostles; that is, that he should not work with his hands, but live by the Gospel, as the Lord appointed, which in what follows he has most openly demonstrated; for to this end did also faithful women which had earthly substance go with them, and minister unto them of their substance, that they might lack none of those things which pertain to the necessities of this life. Which thing blessed Paul demonstrates to be lawful indeed unto himself, as also the other Apostles did it, but that he had not chosen to use this power he afterwards mentions. This thing some not understanding, have interpreted not "a woman which is a sister," when he said, "Have we not power to lead about a sister a woman;" but, "a sister a wife." They were misled by the ambiguity of the Greek word, because both "wife" and "woman" is expressed in Greek by the same word. Though indeed the Apostle has so put this that they ought not to have made this mistake; for that he neither says "a woman" merely, but "a sister woman;" nor "to take" (as in marriage), but "to take about" (as on a journey). Howbeit other interpreters have not been misled by this ambiguity, and they have interpreted "woman" not "wife."

6. Which thing whoso thinks cannot have been done by the Apostles, that with them women of holy conversation should go about wheresoever they preached the Gospel, that of their substance they might minister to

their necessities, let him hear the Gospel, and learn how in this they did after the example of the Lord Himself. Our Lord, namely, according to the wont of His pity, sympathizing with the weak, albeit Angels might minister unto Him, had both a bag in which should be put the money which was bestowed doubtless by good and believing persons, as necessary for their living, (which bag He gave in charge to Judas, that even thieves, if we could not keep clear of such, we might learn to tolerate in the Church. He, namely, as is written of him, "stole2488what was put therein:") and He willed that women should follow Him for the preparing and ministering what was necessary, showing what was due to evangelists and ministers of God as soldiers, from the people of God as the provincials; so that if any should not choose to use that which is due unto him, as Paul the Apostle did not choose, he might bestow the more upon the Church, by not exacting the pay which was due to him, but by earning his daily living of his own labors. For it had been said to the inn-keeper to whom that wounded man was brought, "Whatever thou lays out more, at my coming again I will repay thee." The Apostle Paul, then, did "lay out more," in that he, as himself witnessed, did at his own charges go a warfare. In the Gospel, namely, it is written, "Thereafter also Himself was making a journey through cities and villages preaching and evangelizing of the kingdom of God; and the twelve with Him, and certain women which had been healed of evil spirits and infirmities: Mary who is called Magdalene, out of whom seven devils had gone forth, and Joanna wife of Chuza Herod's steward, and Susanna, and many others, who ministered unto Him of their substance." This example of the Lord the Apostles did imitate, to receive the meat which was due unto them; of which the same Lord most openly speaks: "As ye go," saith He, "preach, saying, The kingdom of heaven is at hand. Heal the sick, raise the dead, cleanse lepers, cast out devils. Freely have ye received, freely give. Possess not gold nor silver nor money in your purses, neither scrip on your journey, neither two coats, neither shoes, neither staff: for the workman is worthy of his meat." Lo, where the Lord appointed the very thing which the Apostle doth mention. For to this end He told them not to carry all those things, namely, that where need should be, they might receive them of them unto whom they preached the kingdom of God.

7. But lest any should fancy that this was granted only to the twelve, see also what Luke related: "After these things," saith he, "the Lord chose also other seventy and two, and sent them by two and two before His face into every city and place whither He was about to come. And He said unto them, The harvest indeed is plentiful, but the laborers few: ask ye therefore the Lord of the harvest, that He would send forth laborers into His harvest. Go your ways: behold, I send you as lambs in the midst of wolves. Carry neither purse nor scrip nor shoes, and salute no man by the way. Into whatsoever house ye shall enter, first say, Peace be to this house. And if the son of peace be there, your peace shall rest upon him: if not, it shall return to you. And in the same house remain, eating and drinking such things as are with them: for the workman is worthy of his hire." Here it appears that these things were not commanded, but permitted, that whoso should choose to use, might use that which was lawful unto him by the Lord's appointment; but if any should not

choose to use it, he would not do contrary to a thing commanded, but would be yielding up his own right, by demeaning himself more mercifully and laboriously in the Gospel in the which he would not accept even the hire which was his due. Otherwise the Apostle did contrary to a command of the Lord: for, after he had shown it to be lawful unto him, he hath straightway subjoined, "But yet have I not used this power."

8. But let us return to the order of our discourse, and the whole of the passage itself of the Epistle let us diligently consider. "Have we not," saith he, "leave to eat and to drink? have we not leave to lead about a woman, a sister?" What leave meant he, but what the Lord gave unto them whom He sent to preach the kingdom of heaven, saying, "Those things which are (given) of them, eat ye; for the workman is worthy of his hire;" and proposing Himself as an example of the same power, to Whom most faithful women did of their means minister such necessaries? But the Apostle Paul hath done more, from his fellow-Apostles alleging a proof of this license permitted of the Lord. For not as finding fault hath he subjoined, "As do also the other Apostles, and the brethren of the Lord, and Cephas;" but that hence he might show that this which he would not accept was a thing which, that it was lawful for him to accept was proved by the wont of the rest also his fellow-soldiers. "Or I only and Barnabas, have we not power to forbear working?" Lo, he hath taken away all doubt even from the slowest hearts, that they may understand of what working he speaks. For to what end saith he, "Or I only and Barnabas, have we not power to forbear working?" but for that all evangelists and ministers of God's word had

power received of the Lord, not to work with their hands, but to live by the Gospel, working only spiritual works in preaching of the kingdom of heaven and edifying of the peace of the Church? For no man can say that it is of that very spiritual working that the Apostle said, "Or I only and Barnabas, have we not power to forbear working?" For this power to forbear working all those had: let him say then, who essays to deprave and pervert precepts Apostolical; let him say, if he dares that all evangelists received of the Lord power to forbear preaching the Gospel. But if this is most absurd and mad to say, why will they not understand what is plain to all, that they did indeed receive power not to work, but works bodily, whereby to get a living, because "the workman is worthy of his hire," as the Gospel speaks. It is not therefore that Paul and Barnabas only had not power to forbear working; but that all alike had this power of which these availed not themselves in "laying out more" upon the Church; so as in those places where they preached the Gospel they judged to be meet for the weak. And for this reason, that he might not seem to have found fault with his fellow-Apostles, he goes on to say: "Who goes a warfare at any time at his own charges? Who fed a flock, and of the milk of the flock partakes not? Speak I these things as a man? Saith not the Law the same? For in the law of Moses it is written, Thou shall not muzzle the ox that treaded out the corn. Doth God care for oxen? Or saith he it for our sake altogether? For our sakes truly is it written, because he that ploughed ought to plough in hope, and he that threshed in hope of partaking of the fruits." By these words the Apostle Paul sufficiently indicates, that it was no usurping unto themselves of aught beyond their due on the part of his fellow-Apostles, that they wrought not bodily, whence they might have the things which to this life are necessary, but as the Lord ordained, should, living by the Gospel, eat bread gratuitously given of them unto whom they were preaching a gratuitous grace. Their charges, namely, they did like soldiers receive, and of the fruit of the vineyard by them planted, they did, as need was, freely gather; and of the milk of the flock which they fed, they drank; and of the threshing floor on which they threshed, they took their meat.

9. But he speaks more openly in the rest which he subjoins, and altogether removes all causes of doubting. "If we unto you," saith he, "have sown spiritual things, is it a great matter if we shall reap your carnal things?" What are the spiritual things which he sowed, but the word and mystery of the sacrament of the kingdom of heaven? And what the carnal things which he saith he had a right to reap, but these temporal things which are indulged to the life and indigency of the flesh? These however being due to him he declares that he had not sought nor accepted, lest he should cause any impediment to the Gospel of Christ. What work remained for us to understand him to have wrought, whereby he should get his living, but bodily work, with his own bodily and visible hands? For if from spiritual work he sought food and clothing, that is, to receive these of them whom he was edifying in the Gospel, he could not, as he does, go on to say, "If others be partakers of this power over you, are not we rather? Nevertheless, we have not used this power, but tolerate all things that we may not cause any hindrance to the Gospel of Christ." What power doth he say he had not used, but that which he had over them,

received of the Lord, the power to reap their carnal things, in order to the sustenance of this life which is lived in the flesh? Of which power were others also partakers, who did not at the first announce the Gospel to them, but came thereafter to their Church preaching the self-same. Therefore, when he had said, "If we have sown unto you spiritual things, is it a great matter if we shall reap your carnal things?" he subjoined, "If others be partakers of this power over you, are not we rather?" And when he had demonstrated what power they had: "Nevertheless we have not used," saith he, "this power; but we put up with all things, lest we should cause any impediment to the Gospel of Christ." Let therefore these persons say in what way from spiritual work the Apostle had carnal food, when himself openly says that he had not used this power. But if from spiritual work he had not carnal food, it remains that from bodily work he had it and thereof saith, "Neither did we eat any man's bread for naught; but wrought with labor and travail night and day, that we might not be chargeable to any of you: not because we have not power, but to make ourselves an example unto you to follow us. All things," saith he, "we suffer, lest we cause any hindrance to the Gospel of Christ."

10. And he comes back again, and in all ways, over and over again, enforces what he hath the right to do, yet doeth not. "Do ye not know," saith he, "that they which work in the temple, eat of the things which are in the temple? they which serve the altar, have their share with the altar? So hath the Lord ordained for them which preach the Gospel, to live of the Gospel. But I have used none of these things." What more open than this? what clearer? I fear lest haply, while I discourse wishing to

expound this, that become obscure which in itself is bright and clear. For they who understand not these words, or feign not to understand, do much less understand mine, or profess to understand: unless perchance they do therefore quickly understand ours, because it is allowed them to deride them being understood; but concerning the Apostle's words this same is not allowed. For this reason, where they cannot interpret them otherwise according to their own sentence, be it ever so clear and manifest, they answer that it is obscure and uncertain because wrong and perverse they dare not call it. Cries the man of God, "The Lord hath ordained for them which preach the Gospel, of this Gospel to live; but I have used none of these things;" and flesh and blood essayed to make crooked what is straight; what open, to shut; what serene, to cloud over. "It was," saith it, "spiritual work that he was doing, and thereof did he live." If it be so, of the Gospel did he live: why then doth he say, "The Lord hath ordained for them which preach the Gospel, of the Gospel to live; but I have used none of these things?" Or if this very word, "to live" which is here used, they will needs also interpret in respect of spiritual life, then had the Apostle no hope towards God, in that he did not live by the Gospel, because he hath said, "I have used none of these things." Wherefore, that he should have certain hope of life eternal the Apostle did of the Gospel in any wise spiritually live. What therefore he saith, "But I have used none of these things," doth without doubt make to be understood of this life which is in the flesh, that which he hath said of the Lord's ordaining to them which preach the Gospel, that of the Gospel they should live; that is, this life which hath need of food and clothing, they by the Gospel shall sustain; as above he said of his fellow apostles; of whom the Lord Himself saith, "The workman is worthy of his meat;" and, "The workman is worthy of his hire." This meat, then, and this hire of the sustenance of this life, due to evangelists, this of them to whom he evangelized the Apostle accepted not, saying a true thing, "I have used none of these things."

11. And he goes on, and adjoins, lest perchance any should imagine that he only therefore received not, because they had not given: "But I have not written these things that they may be so done unto me: good is it for me rather to die than that any make void my glory." What glory, unless that which he wished to have with God, while in Christ suffering with the weak? As he is presently about to say most openly; "For if I shall have preached the Gospel, there is not to me any glory: for necessity is laid upon me;" that is, of sustaining this life. "For woe will be to me," he saith, "if I preach not the Gospel:" that is, to my own will shall I forbear to preach the Gospel, because I shall be tormented with hunger, and shall not have whereof to live. For he goes on, and says; "For if willingly I do this, I have a reward." By his doing it willingly, he means, if he do it uncompelled by any necessity of supporting this present life; and for this he hath reward, to wit, with God, of glory everlasting. "But if unwilling," saith he, "a dispensation is entrusted unto me:" that is, if being unwilling, I am by necessity of passing through this present life, compelled to preach the Gospel, "a dispensation is entrusted unto me;" to wit, that by my dispensation as a steward, because Christ, because the truth, is that which I preach, howsoever because of occasion, howsoever seeking mine own, howsoever by necessity of earthly emolument compelled so to do, other

men do profit, but I have not that glorious and everlasting reward with God. "What then," saith he, "shall be my reward?" He saith it as asking a question: therefore the pronunciation must be suspended, until he give the answer. Which the more easily to understand, let, as it were, us put the question to him, "What, then, will be thy reward, O Apostle, when that earthly reward due to good evangelists, not for its sake evangelizing, but yet taking it as the consequence and offered to them by the Lord's appointment, thou accepts not? What shall be thy reward then?" See what he replies: "That, preaching the Gospel, I may make the Gospel of Christ without charge;" that is, that the Gospel may not be to believers expensive, lest they account that for this end is the Gospel to be preached to them, that its preachers should seem as it were to sell it. And yet he comes back again and again, that he may show what, by warrant of the Lord, he hath a right unto, yet doeth not: "that I abuse not," saith he, "my power in the Gospel."

12. But now, that as bearing with the infirmity of men he did this, let us hear what follows: "For though I be free from all men, yet have I made myself servant unto all, that I might gain the more. To them that are under the law, I became as under the law, that I might gain them that are under the law; to them that are without law, as without law, (being not without law to God, but under the law to Christ,) that I might gain them that are without law." Which thing he did, not with craftiness of simulation, but with mercy of compassion with others; that is, not as if to feign himself a Jew, as some have thought, in that he observed at Jerusalem the things prescribed by the old law. For he did this in accordance

with his free and openly declared sentence, in which he says, "Is any called being circumcised? let him not become uncircumcised." That is, let him not so live, as though he had become uncircumcised, and covered that which he had laid bare: as in another place he saith, "Thy circumcision is become uncircumcision." It was in accordance then with this his sentence, in which he saith, "Is any called being circumcised? let him not become uncircumcised. Is any called in uncircumcision? let him not be circumcised;" that he did those things, in which, by persons not understanding and not enough attending, he has been accounted to have feigned. For he was a Jew, and was called being circumcised; therefore he would not become uncircumcised; that is, would not so live as if he had not been circumcised. For this he now had in his power to do. And "under" the law, indeed, he was not as they who servilely wrought it; but yet "in" the law of God and of Christ. For that law was not one, and the law of God another, as accursed Manicheans are wont to say. Otherwise, if when he did those things he is to be accounted to have feigned, then he feigned himself also a pagan, and sacrificed to idols, because he says that he became to those without law, as without law. By whom, doubtless, he would have us to understand no other than Gentiles whom we call Pagans. It is one thing therefore to be under the law, another in the law, another without law. "Under the law," the carnal Jews; "in the law," spiritual men, both Jews and Christians; (whence the former kept that custom of their fathers, but did not impose unwonted burdens upon the believing Gentiles; and therefore they also were circumcised;) but "without law," are the Gentiles which have not yet believed, to whom yet the Apostle testified himself to have become like, through sympathy of a merciful heart, not simulation of a changeable exterior; that is, that he might in that way succor carnal Jew or Pagan, in which way himself, if he were that, would have wished to be succored: bearing, to wit, their infirmity, in likeness of compassion, not deceiving in fiction of lying; as he straightway goes on, and says, "I became to the weak as weak, that I might gain the weak." For it was from this point that he was speaking, in saying all those other things. As then, that he became to the weak as weak, was no lie; so all those other things above rehearsed. For what doth he mean his weakness towards the weak to have been, but that of suffering with them, insomuch that, lest he should appear to be a seller of the Gospel, and by falling into an ill suspicion with ignorant men, should hinder the course of God's word, he would not accept what by warrant of the Lord was his due? Which if he were willing to accept, he would not in any wise lie, because it was truly due to him; and for that he would not, he did not in any wise lie. For he did not say, it was not due; but he showed it to be due, and that being due he had not used it, and professed that he would not at all use it, in that very thing becoming weak; namely, in that he would not use his power; being, to wit, with so merciful affection endued, that he thought in what way he should wish to be dealt withal, if himself also were made so weak, that possibly, if he should see them by whom the Gospel was preached to him, accepting their charges, he might think it a bringing of wares to market, and hold them in suspicion accordingly.

13. Of this weakness of his, he saith in another place, "We made ourselves small among you, even as a nurse cherished her children." For in that passage the

context indicates this: "For neither at any time," saith he, "used we flattering words, as ye know, nor an occasion of covetousness; God is witness: nor of men sought we glory, neither of you, nor yet of others when we might have been burdensome to you as the Apostles of Christ: but we made ourselves small among you, even as a nurse cherished her children." What therefore he saith to the Corinthians, that he had power of his apostleship, as also the other Apostles, which power he testified that he had not used; this also he saith in that place to the Thessalonians, "When we might have been burdensome to you as Christ's Apostles:" according to that the Lord saith, "The workman is worthy of his hire." For that of this he speaks, is indicated by that which he above set down, "Neither for occasion of coveteousness, God is witness." By reason, namely, of this which by right of the Lord's appointment was due to good evangelists, who not for its sake do evangelize but seek the kingdom of God, so that all these things should be added unto them, others were taking advantage thereof, of whom he also saith, "For they that are such serve not God, but their own belly." From whom the Apostle wished so to cut off this occasion, that even what was justly due to him, he would forego. For this himself doth openly show in the second to the Corinthians, speaking of other Churches supplying his necessities. For he had come, as it appears, to so great indigence, that from distant Churches were sent supplies for his necessities, while yet from them among whom he was, he accepted nothing of that kind. "Have I committed a sin, "saith he, "in humbling myself that ye might be exalted, because I have preached to you the Gospel of God freely? Other Churches I despoiled, taking wages of them to minister unto you: and when I was present with you and wanted, to no man was I burdensome. For that which was lacking to me the brethren which came from Macedonia supplied, and in all things I have kept myself from being burdensome to you, and will keep myself. It is the truth of Christ in me, that this glory shall not be infringed in me in the regions of Achaia. Wherefore? because I love you not? God knows. But what I do, I also mean to do, that I may cut off occasion from them which seek occasion, that wherein they glory they may be found as also we." Of this occasion, therefore, which he here saith that he cuts off, he would have that understood which he saith in the former place, "Neither for occasion of covetousness, God is witness." And what he here saith, "In humbling myself that ye might be exalted:" this in the first to the same Corinthians, "I became to the weak as weak;" this to the Thessalonians, "I became small among you, as a nurse cherished her children." Now then observe what follows: "So," saith he, "being affectionately desirous of you, we are minded to impart unto you not alone the Gospel of God, but our own souls also; because ye are become most dear to us. For ye remember, brethren, our labor and toil, night and day working, that we might not burden any of you." For this he said above, "When we might be burdensome to you, as Christ's Apostles." Because, then, the weak were in peril, lest, agitated by false suspicions, they should hate an, as it were, venal Gospel, for this cause, trembling for them as with a father's and a mother's bowels of compassion, did he this thing. So too in the Acts of the Apostles he speaks the same thing, when, sending from Miletus to Ephesus, he had called thence the presbyters of the Church, to whom, among much else, "Silver," saith he, "and gold, or apparel of no man have I coveted; yourselves know, that to my necessities and theirs who were with me these hands have ministered. In all things have I shown you that so laboring it behooves to help the weak, mindful also of the words of the Lord Jesus, for that He said, More blessed is it rather to give than to receive.

14. Here peradventure some man may say, "If it was bodily work that the Apostle wrought, whereby to sustain this life, what was that same work, and when did he find time for it, both to work and to preach the Gospel?" To whom I answer: Suppose I do not know; nevertheless that he did bodily work, and thereby lived in the flesh, and did not use the power which the Lord had given to the Apostles, that preaching the Gospel he should live by the Gospel, those things above-said do without all doubt bear witness. For it is not either in one place or briefly said, that it should be possible for any most astute arguer with all his tergiversation to traduce and pervert it to another meaning. Since then so great an authority, with so mighty and so frequent blows mauling the gainsayers, doth break in pieces their contrariness, why ask they of me either what sort of work he did, or when he did it? One thing I know, that he neither did steal, nor was a housebreaker or highwayman, nor chariot driver or hunter or player, nor given to filthy lucre: but innocently and honestly wrought things which are fitted for the uses of men; such as are the works of carpenters, builders, shoemakers, peasants, and such like. For honesty itself reprehends not what their pride doth reprehend, who love to be called, but love not to be, honest. The Apostle then would not disdain either to take in hand any work of peasants, or to be employed in the labor of craftsmen. For he who saith, "Be ye without offense to Jews and to

Greeks and to the Church of God," before what men he could possibly stand abashed, I know not. If they shall say, the Jews; the Patriarchs fed cattle: if the Greeks, whom we call also Pagans; they have had philosophers, held in high honor, who were shoemakers: if the Church of God; that just man, elect to the testimony of a conjugal and ever-during virginity, to whom was betrothed the Virgin Mary who bore Christ, was a carpenter. Whatever therefore of these with innocence and without fraud men do work, is good. For the Apostle himself takes precaution of this, that no man through necessity of sustaining life should turn aside to evil works. "Let him that stole," saith he, "steal no more; but rather let him labor good with his hands, that he may have to impart to him that needed." This then is enough to know, that also in the very work of the body the Apostle did work that which is good.

15. But when he might use to work, that is, in what spaces of time, that he might not be hindered from preaching the Gospel, who can make out? Though, truly, that he wrought at hours of both day and night himself hath not left untold. Yet these men truly, who as though very full of business and occupation inquire about the time of working, what do they? Have they from Jerusalem round about even to Illyricum filled the lands with the Gospel? or whatever of barbarian nations hath remained yet to be gone unto, and to be filled of the peace of the Church, have they undertaken? We know them into a certain holy society, most leisurely gathered together. A marvelous thing did the Apostle, that in very deed amid his so great care of all the Churches, both planted and to be planted, to his care and labor appertaining, he did also

with his hands work: yet on that account, when he was with the Corinthians, and wanted, was burdensome to no man of those among whom he was, but altogether that which was lacking to him the brethren which came from Macedonia supplied.

16. For he himself also, with an eye to the like necessities of saints, who, although they obey his precepts, "that with silence they work and eat their own bread," may yet from many causes stand in need of somewhat by way of supplement to the like sustenance, therefore, after he had thus said, teaching and premonishing, "Now them which are such we command and beseech in our Lord Jesus Christ, that with silence they work and eat their own bread;" yet, lest they which had whereof they might supply the needs of the servants of God, should hence take occasion to wax lazy, providing against this he hath straightway added, "But ye, brethren, become not weak in showing beneficence." And when he was writing to Titus, saying, "Zenas the lawyer and Apollos do thou diligently send forward, that nothing may be wanting to them;" that he might show from what quarter nothing ought to be wanting to them, he straightway subjoined, "But let ours also learn to maintain good works for necessary use, that they be not unfruitful." In the case of Timothy also, whom he calls his own most true son, because he knew him weak of body, (as he shows, in advising him not to drink water, but to use a little wine for his stomach's sake and his often infirmities,) lest then haply, because in bodily work he could not labor, he being unwilling to stand in need of daily food at their hands, unto whom he ministered the Gospel, should seek some business in which the stress of

his mind would become entangled; (for it is one thing to labor in body, with the mind free, as does a handicraftsman, if he be not fraudulent and avaricious and greedy of his own private gain; but another thing, to occupy the mind itself with cares of collecting money without the body's labor, as do either dealers, or bailiffs, or undertakers, for these with care of the mind conduct their business, not with their hands do work, and in that regard occupy their mind itself with solicitude of getting;) lest then Timothy should fall upon such like ways, because from weakness of body he could not work with his hands, he thus exhorts, admonishes, and comforts him: "Labor," saith he, "as a good soldier of Jesus Christ. No man, going a warfare for God, entangled himself with secular business; that he may please Him to whom he hath proved himself. For he that strives for masteries, is not crowned except he strives lawfully." Hereupon, lest the other should be put to straits, saying, "Dig I cannot, to beg I am ashamed," he adjoined, "The husbandman that labored must be first partaker of the fruits:" according to that which he had said to the Corinthians, "Who goes a warfare any time at his own charges? Who planted a vineyard, and eat not of the fruit thereof? Who feeds a flock, and partakes not of the milk of the flock?" Thus did he make to be without care a chaste evangelist, not to that end working as an evangelist that he might sell the Gospel, but yet not, having strength to supply unto himself with his own hands the necessities of this life; for that he should understand whatever being necessary for himself he was taking of them whom as provincials he as a soldier was serving, and whom as a vineyard he was culturing, or as a flock was feeding, to be not matter of mendicity, but of power.

17. On account then of these either occupations of the servants of God, or bodily infirmities, which cannot be altogether wanting, not only doth the Apostle permit the needs of saints to be supplied by good believers, but also most wholesomely exhorted. For, setting apart that power, which he saith himself had not used, which yet that the faithful must serve unto, he enjoins, saying, "Let him that is catechized in the word, communicate unto him that doth catechize him, in all good things:" setting apart, then, this power, which that the preachers of the word have over them to whom they preach, he often testified; speaking, moreover, of the saints who had sold all that they had and distributed the same, and were dwelling at Jerusalem in an holy communion of life, not saying that anything was their own, to whom all things were in common, and their soul and heart one in the Lord: that these by the Churches of the Gentiles should have what they needed bestowed upon them, he charged and exhorted. Thence is also that to the Romans: "Now therefore I will go unto Jerusalem, to minister unto the saints. For it hath pleased Macedonia and Achaia to make a certain contribution for the poor of the saints which are at Jerusalem. For it hath pleased them; and their debtors they are. For if in their spiritual things the Gentiles have communicated, they ought also in carnal things to minister unto them." This is like that which he says to the Corinthians: "If we have sown unto you spiritual things, is it a great thing if we reap your carnal things?" Also to the Corinthians in the second Epistle: "Moreover, brethren, we do you to wit of the grace of God bestowed on the Churches of Macedonia; how that in a great trial of affliction the abundance of their joy and their deep poverty abounded in the riches of their liberality; for to

their power, I bear record, yea, and beyond their power, they were willing of themselves; with many prayers beseeching of us the grace and the fellowship of the ministering to the saints: and not as we hoped, but first they gave their own selves to the Lord, and unto us by the will of God, insomuch, that we desired Titus, that as he had begun, so he would also finish in you the same grace also. But as ye abound in everything, in faith, and utterance, and knowledge, and in all diligence, and in your love to us, see that ye abound in this grace also. I speak not by commandment, but by occasion of the forwardness of others, and to prove the exceeding dearness of your love. For ye know the grace of our Lord Jesus Christ, that, though He was rich, yet for your sakes He became poor, that ye through His poverty might be made rich. And herein I give advice: for this is expedient for you, who have begun before, not only to do, but also to be willing a year ago; now therefore perfect it in the doing; that as there is a readiness to will, so of performance also out of that which each hath. For if there be first a ready mind, it is acceptable according to that a man hath, not according to that he hath not. Not, namely, that others may have ease, and ye straits; but by an equality, that now at this time your abundance may be a supply for their want, that their abundance also may become a supply for your want: that there may be equality, as it is written, He that had gathered much had nothing over; and he that had gathered little had no lack. But thanks be to God, which put the same earnest care for you into the heart of Titus: for indeed he accepted the exhortation; but being more forward, of his own accord he went forth unto you. And we have sent with him the brother, whose praise is in the Gospel throughout all the

Churches; and not that only, but he was also ordained of the Churches as a companion of our travail, with this grace which is administered by us to the glory of the Lord, and our ready mind: avoiding this, that no man should blame us in this abundance which is administered by us. For we provide for honest things, not only in the sight of the Lord, but also in the sight of men." In these words appeared how much the Apostle willed it not only to be the care of the holy congregations to minister necessaries to the holy servants of God, giving counsel in this, because this was profitable more to the persons themselves who did this, than to them towards whom they did it, (for to those another thing was profitable, that is, that they should make of this service of their brethren towards them an holy use, and not with an eye to this serve God, nor take these things but to supply necessity, not to feed laziness:) but likewise his own care the blessed Apostle saith to be so great in this ministration which was now in transmitting through Titus, that a companion of his journey was on this account, he tells us, ordained by the Churches, a man of God well reported of, "whose praise," says he, "is in the Gospel throughout all the Churches." And to this end, he says, was the same ordained to be his companion, that he might avoid men's reprehensions, lest, without witness of saints associated with him in this ministry, he should be thought by weak and impious men to receive for himself and turn aside into his own bosom, what he was receiving for supplying the necessities of the saints, by him to be brought and distributed to the needy.

18. And a little after he saith, "For as touching the ministering to the saints, it is superfluous for me to write to you. For I know the forwardness of your mind, for

which I boast of you to them of Macedonia, that Achaia was ready a year ago; and your zeal hath provoked very many. Yet have we sent the brethren, lest our boasting of you should be in vain in this behalf; that, as I said, ye may be ready: lest haply if they of Macedonia come with me, and find you unprepared, we (that we say not, ye) should be ashamed in this substance. Therefore I thought it necessary to exhort the brethren, that they would go before unto you, and make up beforehand this your long promised benediction, that the same might be ready, as benediction, and not as covetousness. But this I say, He which soweth sparingly shall reap also sparingly; and he which soweth in benediction shall reap also in benediction. Every man according as he hath purposed in his heart, not grudgingly, or of necessity: for God loveth a cheerful giver. And God is able to make all grace abound in you; that ye, always having all sufficiency in all things, may abound to every good work: as it is written, He hath dispersed abroad; he hath given to the poor: his righteousness remained forever. But He that ministered seed to the sower will both minister bread for your food, and multiply your seed sown, and increase the growing fruits of your righteousness; that ye may be enriched in everything to all bountifulness, which caused through us thanksgiving to God: for the administration of this service not only supplied the want of the saints, but makes them also to abound by thanksgiving unto God of many, while by the proof of this ministration they glorify God for the obedience of your confession unto the Gospel of Christ, and for your liberal distribution unto them, and unto all men; and in the praying for you of them which long after you for the excellent grace of God in you. Thanks be unto God for His unspeakable gift." In what richness of holy gladness must the Apostle have been steeped, while he speaks of the mutual supply of the need of Christ's soldiers and His other subjects, on the one part of carnal things to those, on the other of spiritual things to these, to exclaim as he does, and as it were in repletion of holy joys to burst out with, "Thanks be to God for His unspeakable gift!"

19. As therefore the Apostle, nay rather the Spirit of God possessing and filling and actuating his heart, ceased not to exhort the faithful who had such substance, that nothing should be lacking to the necessities of the servants of God, who wished to hold a more lofty degree of sanctity in the Church, in cutting off all ties of secular hope, and dedicating a mind at liberty to their godly service of warfare: likewise ought themselves also to obey his precepts, in sympathizing with the weak, and unshackled by love of private wealth, to labor with their hands for the common good, and submit to their superiors without a murmur; that there may be made up for them out of the oblations of good believers that which, while they labor and do some work whereby they may get their living, yet still by reason of bodily infirmities of some, and by reason of ecclesiastical occupations or erudition of the doctrine which brings salvation, they shall account to be lacking.

20. For what these men are about, who will not do bodily work, to what thing they give up their time, I should like to know. "To prayers," say they, "and psalms, and reading, and the word of God." A holy life, unquestionably, and in sweetness of Christ worthy of praise; but then, if from these we are not to be called off,

Of the Work of Monks

neither must we eat, nor our daily viands themselves be prepared, that they may be put before us and taken. Now if to find time for these things the servants of God at certain intervals of times by very infirmity are of necessity compelled, why do we not make account of some portions of times to be allotted also to the observance of Apostolical precepts? For one single prayer of one who obeys is sooner heard than ten thousand of a despiser. As for divine songs, however, they can easily, even while working with their hands, say them, and like as rowers with a boat-song, so with godly melody cheer up their very toil. Or are we ignorant how it is with all workmen, to what vanities, and for the most part even filthinesses, of theatrical fables they give their hearts and tongues, while their hands recede not from their work? What then hinders a servant of God while working with his hands to meditate in the law of the Lord, and sing unto the Name of the Lord Most High? provided, of course, that to learn what he may by memory rehearse, he have times set apart. For to this end also those good works of the faithful ought not to be lacking, for resource of making up what is necessary, that the hours which are so taken up in storing of the mind that those bodily works cannot be carried on, may not oppress with want. But they which say that they give up their time to reading, do they not there find that which the Apostle enjoined? Then what perversity is this, to refuse to be ruled by his reading while he wishes to give up his time thereto; and that he may spend more time in reading what is good, therefore to refuse to do what is read? For who knows not that each doth the more quickly profit when he reads good things, the quicker he is in doing what he reads?

21. Moreover, if discourse must be bestowed upon any, and this so take up the speaker that he have not time to work with his hands, are all in the monastery able to hold discourse unto brethren which come unto them from another kind of life, whether it be to expound the divine lessons, or concerning any questions which may be put, to reason in an wholesome manner? Then since not all have the ability, why upon this pretext do all want to have nothing else to do? Although even if all were able, they ought to do it by turns; not only that the rest might not be taken up from necessary works, but also because it sufficed that to many hearers there be one speaker. To come now to the Apostle; how could he find time to work with his hands, unless for the bestowing of the word of God he had certain set times? And indeed God hath not willed this either to be hidden from us. For both of what craft he was a workman, and at what times he was taken up with dispensing the Gospel, holy Scripture has not left untold. Namely, when the day of his departure caused him to be in haste, being at Troas, even on the first day of the week when the brethren were assembled to break bread, such was his earnestness, and so necessary the disputation, that his discourse was prolonged even until midnight, as though it had slipped from their minds that on that day it was not a fast: but when he was making longer stay in any place and disputing daily, who can doubt that he had certain hours set apart for this office? For at Athens, because he had there found most studious inquirers of things, it is thus written of him: "He disputed therefore with the Jews in the synagogue, and with the Gentile inhabitants in the market every day to those who were there." Not, namely, in the synagogue every day, for there it was his custom to discourse on the sabbath; but

"in the market," saith he, "every day;" by reason, doubtless, of the studiousness of the Athenians. For so it follows: "Certain however of the Epicurean and Stoic philosophers conferred with him." And a little after, it says: "Now the Athenians and strangers which were there spent their time in nothing else but either to tell or to hear some new thing." Let us suppose him all those days that he was at Athens not to have worked: on this account, indeed, was his need supplied from Macedonia, as he says in the second to the Corinthians: though in fact he could work both at other hours and of nights, because he was so strong in both mind and body. But when he had gone from Athens, let us see what says the Scripture: "He disputed," saith it, "in the synagogue every sabbath;" this at Corinth. In Troas, however, where through necessity of his departure being close at hand, his discourse was protracted until midnight, it was the first day of the week, which is called the Lord's Day: whence we understand that he was not with Jews but with Christians; when also the narrator himself saith they were gathered together to break bread. And indeed this same is the best management, that all things be distributed to their times and be done in order, lest becoming raveled in perplexing entanglements, they throw our human mind into confusion.

22. There also is said at what work the Apostle wrought. "After these things," it says, "he departed from Athens and came to Corinth; and having found a certain Jew, by name Aquila, of Pontus by birth, lately come from Italy, and Priscilla his wife, because that Claudius had ordered all Jews to depart from Rome, he came unto them, and because he was of the same craft he abode with

them, doing work: for they were tent-makers." This if they shall essay to interpret allegorically, they show what proficient they be in ecclesiastical learning, on which they glory that they bestow all their time. And, at the least, touching those sayings above recited, "Or I only and Barnabas, have we not power to forbear working?" and, "We have not used this power;" and, "When we might be burdensome to you, as Apostles of Christ," and, "Night and day working that we might not burden any of you;" and, "The Lord hath ordained for them which preach the Gospel, of the Gospel to live; but I have used none of these things:" and the rest of this kind, let them either expound otherwise, or if by most clear shining light of truth they be put to it, let them understand and obey; or if to obey they be either unwilling or unable, at least let them own them which be willing, to be better, and them which be also able, to be happier men than they. For it is one thing to plead infirmity of body, either truly alleged, or falsely pretended: but another so to be deceived and so to deceive, that it shall even be thought a proof of righteousness obtaining more mightily in servants of God, if laziness have gotten power to reign among a set of ignorant men. He, namely, who shows a true infirmity of body, must be humanely dealt withal; he who pretends a false one, and cannot be convicted, must be left unto God: yet neither of them fixed a pernicious rule; because a good servant of God both serves his manifestly infirm brother; and, when the other deceives, if he believes him because he does not think him a bad man, he does not imitate him that he may be bad; and if he believe him not; he thinks him deceitful, and does, nevertheless, not imitate him. But when a man says, "This is true righteousness, that by doing no bodily work we imitate the birds of the air, because he who shall do any such work, goes against the Gospel:" whoso being infirm in mind hears and believes this, that person, not for that he so bestows all his time, but for that he so erred, must be mourned over.

23. Hence arises another question; for peradventure one may say, "What then? did the other Apostles, and the brethren of the Lord, and Cephas, sin, in that they did not work? Or did they occasion a hindrance to the Gospel, because blessed Paul saith that he had not used this power on purpose that he might not cause any hindrance to the Gospel of Christ? For if they sinned because they wrought not, then had they not received power not to work, but to live instead by the Gospel. But if they had received this power, by ordinance of the Lord, that they which preach the Gospel should live by the Gospel; and by His saying, "The workman is worthy of his meat;" which power Paul, laying out somewhat more, would not use; then truly they sinned not. If they sinned not, they caused no hindrance. For it is not to be thought no sin to hinder the Gospel. If this be so, "to us also," say they, "it is free either to use or not to use this power."

24. This question I should briefly solve, if I should say, because I should also justly say, that we must believe the Apostle. For he himself knew why in the Churches of the Gentiles it was not meet that a venal Gospel were carried about; not finding fault with his fellow apostles, but distinguishing his own ministry; because they, without doubt by admonition of the Holy Ghost, had so distributed among them the provinces of evangelizing, that Paul and Barnabas should go unto the Gentiles, and they unto the

Circumcision. But that he gave this precept to them who had not the like power, those many things already said do make manifest. But these brethren of ours rashly arrogate unto themselves, so far as I can judge, that they have this kind of power. For if they be evangelists, I confess, they have it: if ministers of the altar, dispensers of sacraments, of course it is no arrogating to themselves, but a plain vindicating of a right.

25. If at the least they once had in this world wherewithal they might easily without handiwork sustain this life, which property, when they were converted unto God, they disparted to the needy, then must we both believe their infirmity, and bear with it. For usually such persons, having been, not better brought up, as many think, but what is the truth, more languidly brought up, are not able to bear the labor of bodily works. Such peradventure were many in Jerusalem. For it is also written, that they sold their houses and lands, and laid the prices of them at the Apostles' feet, that distribution might be made to everyone as he had need. Because they were found, being near, and were useful to the Gentiles, who, being afar off, were thence called from the worship of idols, as it is said, "Out of Zion shall go forth the law, and the word of the Lord from Jerusalem," therefore hath the Apostle called the Christians of the Gentiles their debtors: "their debtors," saith he, "they are:" and hath added the reason why, "For if in their spiritual things the Gentiles have communicated, they ought also in carnal things to minister unto them." But now there come into this profession of the service of God, both persons from the condition of slaves, or also freed-men, or persons on this account freed by their masters or about to be freed,

likewise from the life of peasants, and from the exercise and plebeian labor of handicraftsmen, persons whose bringing up doubtless has been all the better for them, the harder it has been: whom not to admit, is a heavy sin. For many of that sort have turned out truly great men and meet to be imitated. For on this account also "hath God chosen the weak things of the world to confound the things which are mighty, and the foolish things of the world hath He chosen to confound them who are wise; and ignoble things of the world, and things which are not, as though they were, that the things that are may be brought to naught: that no flesh may glory before God." This pious and holy thought, accordingly, caused that even such be admitted as bring no proof of a change of life for the better. For it doth not appear whether they come of purpose for the service of God, or whether running away empty from a poor and laborious life they want to be fed and clothed; yea, moreover, to be honored by them of whom they were wont to be despised and trampled on. Such persons therefore because they cannot excuse themselves from working by pleading infirmity of body, seeing they are convicted by the custom of their past life, do therefore shelter themselves under the screen of an ill scholarship, that from the Gospel badly understood they should essay to pervert precepts apostolical: truly "fowls of the air," but in lifting themselves on high through pride; and "grass of the field," but in being carnally minded.

26. That, namely, befalls them which in undisciplined younger widows, the same Apostle saith must be avoided: "And withal they learn to be idle; and not only idle, but also busy bodies and full of words,

speaking what they ought not." This very thing said he concerning evil women, which we also in evil men do mourn and bewail, who against him, the very man in whose Epistles we read these things, do, being idle and full of words, speak what they ought not. And if there be any among them who did with that purpose come to the holy warfare, that they may please Him to whom they have proved themselves, these, when they be so vigorous in strength of body, and soundness of health, that they are able not only to be taught, but also, agreeably unto the Apostle, to work, do, by receiving of these men's idle and corrupt discourses, which they are unable, by reason of their unskilled rawness, to judge of, become changed by pestiferous contagion into the same noisomeness: not only not imitating the obedience of saints which quietly work, and of other monasteries which in most wholesome discipline do live after the apostolic rule; but also insulting better men than themselves, preaching up laziness as the keeper of the Gospel, accusing mercy as the prevaricator therefrom. For a much more merciful work is it to the souls of the weak, to consult for the fair fame of the servants of God, than it is to the bodies of men, to break bread to the hungry. Wherefore I would to God that these, which want to let their hands lie idle, would altogether let their tongues lie idle too. For they would not make so many willing to imitate them, if the examples they set were not merely lazy ones, but mute withal.

27. As it is, however, they, against the Apostle of Christ, recite a Gospel of Christ. For so marvelous are the works of the sluggards, hindered that they want to have that very thing by Gospel, which the Apostle enjoined and

did on purpose that the Gospel itself should not be hindered. And yet, if from the very words of the Gospel we should compel them to live agreeably with their way of understanding it, they will be the first to endeavor to persuade us how they are not to be understood so as they do understand them. For certainly, they say that they therefore ought not to work, for that the birds of the air neither sow nor reap, of which the Lord hath given us a similitude that we should take no thought about such necessaries. Then why do they not attend to that which follows? For it is not only said, that "they sow not, neither reap;" but there is added, "nor gather in apothecas." Now "apothecæ" may be called either "barns," or word for word, "repositories." Then why do these persons want to have idle hands and full repositories? Why do they lay by and keep what they receive of the labors of others, that thereof may be every day somewhat forthcoming? Why, in short, do they grind and cook? For the birds do not this. Or, if they find some whom they may persuade to this work also, namely, to bring unto them day by day viands ready-made; at least their water they either fetch them from springs, or from cisterns and wells draw and set it by: this the fowls do not. But if so please them, let it be the study of good believers and most devoted subjects of the Eternal King, to carry their service to His most valiant soldiers even to that length, that they shall not be forced even to fill a vessel of water for themselves, if now-a-days people have surpassed even them which at that time were at Jerusalem, in a new grade of righteousness, stepping out beyond them. To them, namely, by reason of famine being imminent, and foretold by the Prophets which were at that time, good believers sent out of Greece supplies of corn; of which I suppose they made them bread, or at least procured to be made; which thing the birds do not. But if now-adays these persons, as I began to say, have surpassed these in some grade of righteousness, and do altogether in things pertaining to the maintenance of this life, as do the birds; let them show us men doing such service unto birds as they wish to be done unto them, except indeed birds caught and caged because they are not trusted, lest if they fly they come not back: and yet these would rather enjoy liberty and receive from the fields what is enough, than take their food by men laid before them and made ready.

28. Here then shall these persons in their turn be in another more sublime degree of righteousness outdone, by them who shall so order themselves, that every day they shall betake them into the fields as unto pasture, and at what time they shall find it, pick up their meal, and having allayed their hunger, return. But plainly, on account of the keepers of the fields, how good were it, if the Lord should deign to bestow wings also, that the servants of God being found in other men's fields should not be taken up as thieves, but as starlings be scared off. As things are, however, such a one will do all he can to be like a bird, which the fowler shall not be able to catch. But, lo, let all men allow this to the servants of God, that when they will they should go forth into their fields, and thence depart fearless and refreshed: as it was ordered to the people Israel by the law, that none should lay hands on a thief in his fields, unless he wanted to carry anything away with him from thence; for if he laid hands on nothing but what he had eaten, they would let him go away free and unpunished. Whence also when the disciples of the Lord plucked the ears of corn, the Jews

calumniated them on the score of the sabbath rather than of theft. But how is one to manage about those times of year, at which food that can be taken on the spot is not found in the fields? Whoso shall attempt to take home with him anything which by cooking he may prepare for himself, he shall, according to these persons' understanding of it, be accosted from the Gospel with, "Put it down; for this the birds do not."

29. But let us grant this also, that the whole year round there may in the fields be found either of tree or of herbs or of any manner of roots, that which may be taken as food uncooked; or, at any rate, let so great exercise of body be used, that the things which require cooking, may be taken even raw without hurt, and people may even in winter weather, no matter how rough, go forth to their fodder; and so it shall be the case that nothing be taken away to be prepared, nothing laid up for the morrow. Yet will not those men be able to keep these rules, who for many days separating themselves from sight of men, and allowing none access to them, do shut themselves up, living in great earnestness of prayers. For these do use to shut up with themselves store of aliments, such indeed as are most easily and cheaply had, yet still a store which may suffice for those days during which they purpose that no man shall see them; which thing the birds do not. Now touching these men's exercising of themselves in so marvelous continency, seeing that they have leisure for the doing of these things, and not in proud elation but in merciful sanctity do propose themselves for men's imitation, I not only do not blame it, but know not how to praise it as much as it deserves. And yet what are we to say of such men, according to these persons'

understanding of the evangelical words? Or haply the holier they be, the more unlike are they to the fowls? because unless they lay by for themselves food for many days, to shut themselves up as they do they will not have strength? Howbeit, to them as well as us is it said, "Take therefore no thought for the morrow.

30. Wherefore, that I may briefly embrace the whole matter, let these persons, who from perverse understanding of the Gospel labor to pervert apostolical precepts, either take no thought for the morrow, even as the birds of the air; or let them obey the Apostle, as dear children: yea rather, let them do both, because both accord. For things contrary to his Lord, Paul the servant of Jesus Christ would never advise. This then we say openly to these persons; If the birds of the air ye in such wise understand in the Gospel, that ye will not by working with your hands procure food and clothing; then neither must ye put anything by for the morrow, like as the birds of the air do put nothing by. But if to put somewhat by for the morrow, is possibly not against the Gospel where it is said, "Behold the birds of the air, for they neither sow nor reap nor gather into stores;" then is it possibly not against the Gospel nor against similitude of the birds of the air, to maintain this life of the flesh by labor of corporal working.

31. For if they be urged from the Gospel that they should put nothing by for the morrow, they most rightly answer, "Why then had the Lord Himself a bag in which to put by the money which was collected? Why so long time beforehand, on occasion of impending famine, were

supplies of corn sent to the holy fathers? Why did Apostles in such wise provide things necessary for the indigence of saints lest there should be lack thereafter, that most blessed Paul should thus write to the Corinthians in his Epistle: "Now concerning the collection for the saints, as I have given order to the Churches of Galatia, even so do ye. Upon the first day of the week let every one of you lay by him in store, as God hath prospered him, that the gatherings be not then first made when I come. And when I come, whomsoever ye shall approve by your letters, them will I send to bring your liberality unto Jerusalem. And if it be meet that I go also, they shall go with me?" These and much else they most copiously and most truly bring forward. To whom we answer: Ye see then, albeit the Lord said, "Take no thought for the morrow," yet ye are not by these words constrained to reserve nothing for the morrow: then why do ye say that by the same words ye are constrained to do nothing? Why are the birds of the air not a pattern unto you for reserving nothing, and ye will have them to be a pattern for working nothing?

32. Some man will say: "What then does it profit a servant of God, that, having left the former doings which he had in the world he is converted unto the spiritual life and warfare, if it still behooves him to do business as of a common workman?" As if truly it could be easily unfolded in words, how greatly profited what the Lord, in answer to that rich man who was seeking counsel of laying hold on eternal life, told him to do if he would fain be perfect: sell that he had, distribute all to the indigence of the poor, and follow Him? Or who with so unimpeded course hath followed the Lord, as he who saith, "Not in

vain have I run, nor in vain labored?" who yet both enjoined these works, and did them. This unto us, being by so great authority taught and informed, ought to suffice for a pattern of relinquishing our old resources, and of working with our hands. But we too, aided by the Lord Himself, are able perchance in some sort to apprehend what it doth still profit the servants of God to have left their former businesses, while they do yet thus work. For if a person from being rich is converted to this mode of life, and is hindered by no infirmity of body, are we so without taste of the savor of Christ, as not to understand what an healing it is to the swelling of the old pride, when, having pared off the superfluities by which erewhile the mind was deadly inflamed, he refuses not, for the procuring of that little which is still naturally necessary for this present life, even a common workman's lowly toil? If however he be from a poor estate converted unto this manner of life, let him not account himself to be doing that which he was doing aforetime, if foregoing the love of even increasing his ever so small matter of private substance, and now no more seeking his own but the things which be Jesu Christ's, he hath translated himself into the charity of a life in common, to live in fellowship of them who have one soul and one heart to Godward, so that no man saith that anything is his own, but they have all things common. For if in this earthly commonwealth its chief men in the old times did, as their own men of letters are wont in their most glowing phrase to tell of them, to that degree prefer the common weal of the whole people of their city and country to their own private affairs, that one of them, for subduing of Africa honored with a triumph, would have had nothing to give to his daughter on her marriage, unless by decree of the senate she had been dowered from the public treasury: of what mind ought he to be towards his commonwealth, who is a citizen of that eternal City, the heavenly Jerusalem, but that even what with labor of his own hands he earns, he should have in common with his brother, and if the same lack anything, supply it from the common store; saying with him whose precept and example he hath followed, "As having nothing, and possessing all things?"

33. Wherefore even they which having relinquished or distributed their former, whether ample or in any sort opulent, means, have chosen with pious and wholesome humility to be numbered among the poor of Christ; if they be so strong in body and free from ecclesiastical occupations, (albeit, bringing as they do so great a proof of their purpose, and conferring from their former havings, either very much, or not a little, upon the indigence of the same society, the common fund itself and brotherly charity owes them in return a sustenance of their life,) yet if they too work with their hands, that they may take away all excuse from lazy brethren who come from a more humble condition in life, and therefore one more used to toil; therein they act far more mercifully than when they divided all their goods to the needy. If indeed they be unwilling to do this, who can venture to compel them? Yet then there ought to be found for them works in the monastery, which if more free from bodily exercise, require to be looked unto with vigilant administration, that not even they may eat their bread for naught, because it is now become the common property. Nor is it to be regarded in what monasteries, or in what place, any man may have bestowed his former having upon his indigent brethren. For all Christians make one commonwealth.

And for that cause whoso shall have, no matter in what place, expended upon Christians the things they needed, in what place so ever he also received what himself hath need of, from Christ's goods he doth receive it. Because in what place so ever himself has given to such, who but Christ received it? But, as for them who before they entered this holy society got their living by labor of the body, of which sort are the more part of them which come into monasteries, because of mankind also the more part are such; if they will not work, neither let them eat. For not to that end are the rich, in this Christian warfare, brought low unto piety, that the poor may be lifted up unto pride. As indeed it is by no means seemly that in that mode of life where senators become men of toil, there common workmen should become men of leisure; and whereunto there come, relinquishing their dainties, men who had been masters of houses and lands, there common peasants should be dainty.

34. But then the Lord saith, "Be not solicitous for your life what ye shall eat, nor for the body, what ye shall put on." Rightly: because He had said above, "Ye cannot serve God and mammon." For he who preaches the Gospel with an eye to this, that he may have whereof he may eat and whereof be clothed, accounts that he at the same time both serves God, because he preaches the Gospel; and mammon, because he preaches with an eye to these necessaries: which thing the Lord saith to be impossible. And hereby he who doth for the sake of these things preach the Gospel is convicted that he serves not God but mammon; however God may use him, he knows not how, to other men's advancement. For to this sentence doth He subjoin, saying "Therefore I say unto you, Be not

solicitous for your life what ye shall eat, nor for your body what ye shall put on:" not that they should not procure these things, as much as is enough for necessity, by what means they honestly may; but that they should not look to these things, and for the sake of these do whatever in preaching of the Gospel they are bidden to do. The intention, namely, for which a thing is done, He calls the eye: of which a little above He was speaking with purpose to come down to this, and saying, "The light of thy body is thine eye: if thine eye be single, thy whole body shall be full of light; but if thine eye be evil, thy whole body shall be full of darkness;" that is, such will be thy deeds as shall be thine intention for which thou does them. For indeed that He might come to this, He had before given precept concerning alms, saying, "Lay not up for yourselves treasures on earth where rust and moth doth corrupt, and where thieves break through and steal. But lay up for yourselves treasure in heaven, where neither moth nor rust doth corrupt, and where thieves do not break through nor steal. For where thy treasure shall be, there will thy heart be also." Thereupon He subjoined, "The light of thy body is thine eye:" that they, to wit, which do alms, do them not with that intention that they should either wish to please men, or seek to have repayment on earth of the alms they do. Whence the Apostle, giving charge to Timothy for warning of rich men, "Let them," says he "readily give, communicate, treasure up for themselves a good foundation for the time to come, that they may lay hold on the true life." Since then the Lord hath to the future life directed the eye of them which do alms, and to a heavenly reward, in order that the deeds themselves may be full of light when the eye shall be simple, (for of that last retribution is meant that which He says in another place, "He that received you received Me, and he that received Me received Him that sent Me. He that received a prophet in the name of a prophet shall receive a prophet's reward; and he that received a righteous man in the name of a righteous man shall receive a righteous man's reward. And whosoever shall give to drink unto one of these little ones a cup of cold water only in the name of a disciple, verily I say unto you, his reward shall not be lost,") lest haply after he had reproved the eye of them which bestow things needful upon the indigent both prophets and just men and disciples of the Lord, the eye of the persons to whom these things were done should become depraved, so that for the sake of receiving these things they should wish to serve Christ as His soldiers: "No man," saith He, "can serve two masters." And a little after: "Ye cannot," saith He, "serve God and mammon." And straightway He hath added, "Therefore I say unto you, be not solicitous for your life what ye shall eat, nor for the body what ye shall put on."

35. And that which follows concerning birds of the air and lilies of the field, He saith to this end, that no man may think that God cares not for the needs of His servants; when His most wise Providence reaches unto these in creating and governing those. For it must not be deemed that it is not He that feeds and clothes them also which work with their hands. But lest they turn aside the Christian service of warfare unto their purpose of getting these things, the Lord in this premonished His servants that in this ministry which is due to His Sacrament, we should take thought, not for these, but for His kingdom and righteousness: and all these things shall be added unto

us, whether working by our hands, or whether by infirmity of body hindered from working, or whether bound by such occupation of our very warfare that we are able to do nothing else. For neither does it follow that because the Lord hath said, "Call upon Me in the day of tribulation and I will deliver thee, and thou shalt glorify Me," therefore the Apostle ought not to have fled, and to be let down by the wall in a basket that he might escape the hands of a pursuer, but should rather have waited to be taken, that, like the three children from the midst of the fires, the Lord might deliver him. Or for this reason ought not the Lord either to have said this, "If they shall persecute you in one city, flee ye to another," namely, because He hath said, "If ye shall ask of the Father anything in My name, He will give it you." As then whoever to Christ's disciples when fleeing from persecution should cast up this sort of question, why they did not rather stand, and by calling upon God obtain through His marvelous works in such wise deliverance, as Daniel from the lions, as Peter from his chains, they would answer that they ought not to tempt God, but He would then and then only do the like for them, if it should please Him, when they had nothing that they could do; but when He put flight in their power, although they were thereby delivered, yet were they not delivered but by Him: so likewise to servants of God having time and strength after the example and precept of the Apostle to get their living by their own hands, if any from the Gospel shall raise a question concerning the birds of the air, which sow not nor reap nor gather into stores, and concerning lilies of the field that they toil not neither do they spin; they will easily answer, "If we also, by reason of any either infirmity or occupation cannot work, He will so feed and clothe us, as He doth the birds and the lilies, which do no work of this kind: but when we are able, we ought not to tempt our God; because this very ability of ours, we have it by His gift, and in living by it, we live by His bounty Who hath bounteously bestowed upon us that we should have this ability. And therefore concerning these necessary things we are not solicitous; because when we are able to do these things, He by Whom mankind are fed and clothed doth feed and clothe us: but when we are not able to do these things, He feeds and clothes us by Whom the birds are fed and the lilies clothed, because we are more worth than they. Wherefore in this our warfare, neither for the morrow take we thought: because not for the sake of these temporal things, whereunto pertained To-morrow, but for the sake of those eternal things, where it is evermore To-day, have we proved ourselves unto Him, that, entangled in no secular business, we may please Him.

36. Since these things are so, suffer me awhile, holy brother, (for the Lord giveth me through thee great boldness,) to address these same our sons and brethren whom I know with what love thou together with us dost travail in birth withal, until the Apostolic discipline be formed in them. O servants of God, soldiers of Christ, is it thus ye dissemble the plottings of our most crafty foe, who fearing your good fame, that so goodly odor of Christ, lest good souls should say, "We will run after the odor of thine ointments," and so should escape his snares, and in every way desiring to obscure it with his own stenches, hath dispersed on every side so many hypocrites under the garb of monks, strolling about the provinces, nowhere sent, nowhere fixed, nowhere standing, nowhere

sitting. Some hawking about limbs of martyrs, if indeed of martyrs; others magnifying their fringes and phylacteries; others with a lying story, how they have heard say that their parents or kinsmen are alive in this or that country, and therefore be they on their way to them: and all asking, all exacting, either the costs of their lucrative want, or the price of their pretended sanctity. And in the meanwhile wheresoever they be found out in their evil deeds, or in whatever way they become notorious, under the general name of monks, your purpose is blasphemed, a purpose so good, so holy, that in Christ's name we desire it, as through other lands so through all Africa, to grow and flourish. Then are ye not inflamed with godly jealousy? Does not your heart wax hot within you, and in your meditation a fire kindle, that these men's evil works ye should pursue with good works, that ye should cut off from them occasion of a foul trafficking, by which your estimation is hurt, and a stumbling-block put before the weak? Have mercy then and have compassion, and show to mankind that ye are not seeking in ease a ready subsistence, but through the strait and narrow way of this purpose, are seeking the kingdom of God. Ye have the same cause which the Apostle had, to cut off occasion from them which seek occasion, that they who by their stinks are suffocated, by your good odor may be refreshed.

37. We are not binding heavy burdens and laying them upon your shoulders, while we with a finger will not touch them. Seek out, and acknowledge the labor of our occupations, and in some of us the infirmities of our bodies also, and in the Churches which we serve, that custom now grown up, that they do not suffer us to have

time ourselves for those works to which we exhort you. For though we might say, "Who goes a warfare any time at his own charges? Who planted a vineyard, and eat not of the fruit thereof? Who feeds a flock, and partakes not of the milk of the flock?" yet I call our Lord Jesus, in Whose name I fearlessly say these things, for a witness upon my soul, that so far as it concerns mine own convenience, I would much rather every day at certain hours, as much as is appointed by rule in well-governed monasteries, do some work with my hands, and have the remaining hours free for reading and praying, or some work pertaining to Divine Letters, than have to hear these most annoying perplexities of other men's causes about secular matters, which we must either by adjudication bring to an end, or by intervention cut short. Which troubles the same Apostle hath fastened us withal, (not by his own sentence, but by His who spoke through him,) while yet we do not read that he had to put up with them himself: indeed his was not the sort of work to admit of it, while running to and fro in his Apostleship. Nor hath he said, "If then ye have secular law-suits, bring them before us;" or, "Appoint us to judge them;" but, "Them which are contemptible in the Church, these," saith he, "put ye in place. To your abashment I say it: is it so that there is not among you any wise man who can judge between his brother, but brother goes to law with brother, and that before infidels?" So then wise believers and saints, having their stated abode in the different places, not those who were running hither and hither on the business of the Gospel, were the persons whom he willed to be charged with examination of such affairs. Whence it is nowhere written of him that he on any occasion gave up his time to such matters; from which we are not able to excuse ourselves, even though we be contemptible; because he willed even such to be put in place, in case there were lack of wise men, rather than have the affairs of Christians to be brought into the public courts. Which labor, however, we not without consolation of the Lord take upon us, for hope of eternal life, that we may bring forth fruit with patience. For we are servants unto His Church, and most of all to the weaker members, whatsoever members we in the same body may chance to be. I pass by other innumerable ecclesiastical cares, which perchance no man credits but he who hath experienced the same. Therefore we do not bind heavy burdens and place them on your shoulders, while we ourselves touch them not so much as with a finger; since indeed if with safety to our office we might, (He sees it, Who tries our hearts!) we would rather do these things which we exhort you to do, than the things which we ourselves are forced to do. True it is, to all both us and you, while according to our degree and office we labor, both the way is strait in labor and toil; and yet, while we rejoice in hope, His yoke is easy and His burden light, Who hath called us unto rest, Who passed forth before us from the vale of tears, where not Himself either was without pressure of griefs. If ye be our brethren, if our sons, if we be your fellow servants, or rather in Christ your servants, hear what we admonish, acknowledge what we enjoin, take what we dispense. But if we be Pharisees, binding heavy burdens and laying them on your shoulders; yet do ye the things we say, even though ye disapprove the things we do. But to us it is a very small thing that we be judged by you, or of any human assize. Of how near and dear charity is our care on your behalf, let Him look into it Who hath given what we may offer to be looked into by His eyes. In fine: think what ye will of us: Paul the Apostle enjoins and beseeches you in the Lord, that with silence, that is, quietly and obediently ordered, ye do work and eat your own bread. Of him, as I suppose, ye believe no evil, and He who by him doth speak, on Him have ye believed.

38. These things, my brother Aurelius, most dear unto me, and in the bowels of Christ to be venerated, so far as He hath bestowed on me the ability Who through thee commanded me to do it, touching work of Monks, I have not delayed to write; making this my chief care, lest good brethren obeying apostolic precepts, should by lazy and disobedient be called even prevaricators from the Gospel: that they which work not, may at the least account them which do work to be better than themselves without doubt. But who can bear that contumacious persons resisting most wholesome admonitions of the Apostle, should, not as weaker brethren be borne withal, but even be preached up as holier men; insomuch that monasteries founded on sounder doctrine should be by this double enticement corrupted, the dissolute license of vacation from labor, and the false name of sanctity? Let it be known then to the rest, our brethren and sons, who are accustomed to favor such men, and through ignorance to defend this kind of presumption, that they need themselves most chiefly to be corrected, in order that those may be corrected, nor that they become "weary in well-doing." Truly, in that they do promptly and with alacrity minister unto the servants of God the things they need, not only we blame them not, but we most cordially embrace them: only let them not with perverse mercy more hurt these men's future life, than to their present life they render aid.

39. For there is less sin, if people do not praise the sinner in the desires of his soul, and speak good of him who practices iniquities. Now what is more an iniquity than to wish to be obeyed by inferiors, and to refuse to obey superiors? The Apostle, I mean, not us: insomuch that they even let their hair grow long: a matter, of which he would have no disputing at all, saying, "If any chooses to be contentious, we have no such custom, neither the Church of God. Now this I command;" which gives us to understand that it is not cleverness of reasoning that we are to look for, but authority of one giving command to attend unto. For whereunto, I pray thee, pertained this also, that people so openly against the Apostle's precepts wear long hair? Is it that there must be in such sort vacation, that not even the barbers are to work? Or, because they say that they imitate the Gospel birds, do they fear to be, as it were, plucked, lest they be not able to fly? I shrink from saying more against this fault, out of respect for certain long-haired brethren, in whom, except this, we find much, and well-nigh everything, to venerate. But the more we love them in Christ, the more solicitously do we admonish them. Nor are we afraid indeed, lest their humility reject our admonition; seeing that we also desire to be admonished by such as they, wherever we chance to stumble or to go aside. This then we admonish so holy men, not to be moved by foolish quibblings of vain persons, and imitate in this perversity them whom in all else they are far from resembling. For those persons, hawking about a venal hypocrisy, fear lest shorn sanctity be held cheaper than long-haired; because forsooth he who sees them shall call to mind those ancients whom we read of, Samuel and the rest who did

not cut off their hair. And they do not consider what is the difference between that prophetic veil, and this unveiling which is in the Gospel, of which the Apostle saith, "When thou shall go over unto Christ, the veil shall be taken away." That, namely, which was signified in the veil interposed between the face of Moses and the beholding of the people Israel, that same was also signified in those times by the long hair of the Saints. For the same Apostle saith, that long hair is also instead of a veil: by whose authority these men are hard pressed. Seeing he saith openly, "If a man wear long hair, it is a disgrace to him." "The very disgrace," say they, "we take upon us, for desert of our sins:" holding out a screen of simulated humility, to the end that under cover of it they may carry on their trade of self-importance. Just as if the Apostle were teaching pride when he says, "Every man praying or prophesying with veiled head shamed his head;" and, "A man ought not to veil his head, forsomuch as he is the image and glory of God." Consequently he who says, "Ought not," knows not perchance how to teach humility! However, if this same disgrace in time of the Gospel, which was a thing of a holy meaning in time of Prophecy, be by these people courted as matter of humility, then let them be shorn, and veil their head with haircloth. Only then there will be none of that attracting of people's eyes in which they trade, because Samson was veiled not with haircloth, but with his long hair.

40. And then that further device of theirs, (if words can express it), how painfully ridiculous is it, which they have invented for defense of their long locks! "A man," say they, "the Apostle hath forbidden to have long hair: but then they who have made themselves

eunuchs for the kingdom of God are no longer men." O dotage unparalleled! Well may the person who says this arm himself against Holy Scripture's most manifest proclamations, with counsel of outrageous impiety, and persevere in a tortuous path, and essay to bring in a pestiferous doctrine that not "Blessed is the man who hath not walked in the counsel of the ungodly, and in the way of sinners hath not stood, and in the chair of noisome wickedness hath not sat." For if he would meditate in God's law day and night, there he should find the Apostle Paul himself, who assuredly professing highest chastity saith, "I would that all men were even as I:" and yet shows himself a man, not only in so being, but also in so speaking. For he saith, "When I was a child, I spoke as a child, I understood as a child, I thought as a child; when I became a man, I put away childish things." But why should I mention the Apostle, when concerning our Lord and Savior Himself they know not what they think who say these things. For of Whom but Him is it said, "Until we come all to unity of faith and to knowledge of the Son of God, to the Perfect Man, to the measure of the age of the fullness of Christ; that we be no longer babes, tossed and carried about with every wind of doctrine, in sleight of men, in cunning craftiness for machination of error." With which sleight these persons deceive ignorant people, with which cunning craftiness and machinations of the enemy both they themselves are whirled round, and in their whirling essay to make the minds of the weak which cohere unto them so (in a manner) to spin round with them, that they also may not know where they are. For they have heard or read that which is written, "Whosoever of you have been baptized in Christ, have put on Christ: where is no Jew nor Greek; no bond nor free; no male nor female." And they do not understand that it is in reference to concupiscence of carnal sex that this is said, because in the inner man, wherein we are renewed in newness of our mind, no sex of this kind exists. Then let them not deny themselves to be men, just because in respect of their masculine sex they work not. For wedded Christians also who do this work, are of course not Christians on the score of that which they have in common with the rest who are not Christians and with the very cattle. For that is one thing that is either to infirmity conceded or to mortal propagation paid as a debt, but another that which for the laying hold of incorrupt and eternal life is by faithful profession signified. That then which concerning not veiling of the head is enjoined to men, in the body indeed it is set forth in a figure, but that it is enacted in the mind, wherein is the image and glory of God, the words themselves do indicate: "A man indeed," it saith, "ought not to veil his head, forsomuch as he is the image and glory of God." For where this image is, he doth himself declare, where he saith, "Lie not one to another; but stripping off the old man with his deeds, put ye on the new, which is renewed to the acknowledging of God, according to the image of Him who created him." Who can doubt that this renewing takes place in the mind? But and if any doubt, let him hear a more open sentence. For, giving the same admonition, he thus saith in another place: "As is the truth in Jesus, that ye put off concerning the former conversation the old man, him which is corrupt according to the lust of deception; but be ye renewed in the spirit of your mind, and put on the new man, him which after God is created." What then? Have women not this renewal of mind in which is the image of God? Who would say this? But in the sex of their body they do not signify this; therefore they are bidden to be veiled. The part, namely, which they signify in the very fact of their being women, is that which may be called the concupiscential part, over which the mind bears rule, itself also subjected to its God, when life is most rightly and orderly conducted. What, therefore, in a single individual human being is the mind and the concupiscence, (that ruling, this ruled; that lord, this subject,) the same in two human beings, man and woman, is in regard of the sex of the body exhibited in a figure. Of which sacred import the Apostle speaks when he says, that the man ought not to be veiled, the women ought. For the mind doth the more gloriously advance to higher things, the more diligently the concupiscence is curbed from lower things; until the whole man together with even this now mortal and frail body in the last resurrection be clothed with incorruption and immortality, and death be swallowed up in victory.

41. Wherefore, they which will not do right things, let them give over at least to teach wrong things. Howbeit they be others whom in this speech we reprove: but as for those who by this one fault, of letting their hair contrary to apostolic precept grow long, offend and trouble the Church, because when some being unwilling to think of them anything amiss are forced to twist the manifest words of the Apostle into a wrong meaning, others choose to defend the sound understanding of the Scriptures rather than fawn upon any men, there arise between the weaker and the stronger brethren most bitter and perilous contentions: which things perchance if they knew, these would correct without hesitation this also, in whom we admire and love all else. Those then we not reprove, but

ask and solemnly beseech by the Godhead and the Manhood of Christ and by the charity of the Holy Ghost, that they no more put this stumbling-block before the weak for whom Christ died, and aggravate the grief and torment of our heart when we bethink us how much more readily evil men can imitate this evil thing for deceiving of mankind, when they see this in them whom on the score of other so great good we with deserved offices of Christian love do honor. If however, after this admonition, or rather this solemn entreaty of ours, they shall think fit to persevere in the same, we shall do nothing else but only grieve and mourn. This let them know; it is enough. If they be servants of God, they have pity. If they have not pity, I will not say anything worse. All these things, therefore, in the which peradventure I have been more loquacious than the occupations both of thee and of me could wish, if thou approve the same, make thou to be known to our brethren and sons, on whose behalf thou hast deigned to put this burden upon me: but if aught seem to thee meet to be withdrawn or amended, by reply of your Blessedness I shall know the same.

www.ingramcontent.com/pod-product-compliance
Lightning Source LLC
Chambersburg PA
CBHW052117070526
44584CB00017B/2527